D0448262

If you want hours and hours of fun
AND
If you want to keep your
friends in stitches—
YOU MUST TURN THE PAGES
OF THIS BOOK . . .

the SUPER JOKE BOOK

by

GYLES BRANDRETH

ILLUSTRATED by
NICK BERRINGER

Sterling Publishing Co., Inc.   New York

Other Books by Gyles Brandreth

Biggest Tongue-Twister Book in the World
Brain-Teasers and Mind-Benders
Edward Lear's Book of Mazes
A Game-a-Day Book
A Joke-a-Day Book
Total Nonsense Z to A

Library of Congress Cataloging in Publication Data

Brandreth, Gyles Daubeney, 1948–
    The super joke book.

    "Compiled from the title, 1000 jokes: the greatest
joke book ever known"—Verso t.p.
    Includes index.
    Summary: Hundreds of jokes which are old and new,
hilarious and horrendous.
    1. American wit and humor.   2. Wit and humor,
Juvenile. [1. Jokes]   I. Berringer, Nick, ill.
II. Brandreth, Gyles Daubeney, 1948–   . 1000 jokes,
the greatest joke book ever known.   III. Title.
PN6163.B72   1983   818'.5402   83-397
ISBN 0-8069-4672-5
ISBN 0-8069-4673-3 (lib. bdg.)

ISBN 0-8069-6200-3 (paper)

Published in 1983 by Sterling Publishing Co., Inc.
387 Park Avenue South, New York, N.Y. 10016
The material in this book was compiled from the title, *1000 Jokes: the Greatest
Joke Book Ever Known*, published in Great Britain by Carousel Books, a division
of Transworld Publishers Ltd.
Copyright © 1980 by Gyles Brandreth, illustration copyright © 1980 by
Transworld Publishers Ltd.
Distributed in Canada by Oak Tree Press Ltd.
% Canadian Manda Group, P.O. Box 920,
Station U, Toronto, Ontario M8Z 5P9
Printed in China

Contents

1 Off & Running   7
2 Bad News!   21
3 Funny Folks   31
4 Surprise!   39
5 Excuse Me!   49
6 How Odd . . .   61
7 Oh, No!   71
8 Give & Take   79
9 Show & Tell   91
10 Crazier & Crazier   103
11 Look Out!   115
    Index   125

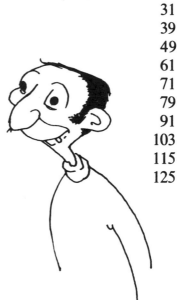

1

Off & Running

BARNEY: I've owned this car for fifteen years and never had a wreck.

PROSPECTIVE BUYER: You mean you've owned this wreck for fifteen years and never had a car.

JUDGE: I've decided to give you a suspended sentence.

PRISONER: Thank you, your honor.

JUDGE: What for? You're going to be hanged.

"Mommy, does God use our
  bathroom?"
"No, darling, why do you ask?"
"Well, every morning Daddy bangs
  on the door and shouts, "Oh,
  God, are you still in there?"

MOTHER: Bobby's teacher says he
  ought to have an encyclopedia.
FATHER: Let him walk to school like I
  had to.

REGGIE: We've got a new dog—
  would you like to come around
  and play with him?
RON: Well, I don't know—does he
  bite?
REGGIE: That's what I want to
  find out.

"Doctor, I keep thinking I'm a goat."
"How long have you had this
feeling?"
"Ever since I was a kid."

MOTHER: Why are you keeping this
box of earth, Willy?
WILLY: That's instant mud-pie mix.

BOY (*howling*): A crab just bit my
toe.
FATHER: Which one?
BOY: How should I know? All
crabs look alike to me.

SAFECRACKER: I think I need
glasses.
MATT: How's that?
SAFECRACKER: Well, I was twirling
the knobs of a safe and an
orchestra began to play.

BOSS (*to Department Head*): How many people work in your office?
DEPT. HEAD: About half of them, sir.

"Why are you scratching yourself, Mary?"
"Because nobody else knows where I itch."

DOCTOR: Good morning, Mrs. Potter, I haven't seen you for a long time.
MRS. POTTER: I know, Doctor, I've been ill.

WAITER: How did you find your chop, sir?
DINER: I looked under a French fry and there it was!

TEACHER: Why do we sometimes call the Middle Ages the Dark Ages?
BETTY: Because they had so many knights.

A little boy saw a grass snake for the first time.
"Mother," he cried, "here's a tail without a body."

TEACHER: Polly, how can you prove the world is round?
POLLY: I never said it was.

A little boy and an old man were standing in the aisle of a crowded bus. "Pass farther down the bus," called the conductor.
"He's not my father," the boy shouted back, "he's my grandfather."

11

CAPTAIN: Why didn't you stop the ball?
GOALIE: I thought that's what the nets were for.

FRANKIE: Which month has twenty-eight days?
PEGGY: All of them.

MIKE: I saw all your chickens out in your front yard yesterday.
PATRICK: Yes, they heard that men were coming to lay a pavement, and they wanted to see how it was done.

MOTHER: Bobby, have you given the goldfish fresh water today?
BOBBY: No, they haven't finished what I gave them yesterday.

TOMMY: Dad, what are four grapes and three grapes?

DAD: Don't you know simple arithmetic? Haven't you done a problem like that before?

TOMMY: No, Dad, we always use bananas at school.

"Doctor—I can't get to sleep at night."

"Don't worry—just lie on the edge of the bed and soon you'll drop off."

"Waiter, there's a dead fly in my soup."

"Yes, sir, I know—it's the heat that kills them."

BIG MAN (*in a theater, to a small boy sitting behind him*): Can you see, sonny?

BOY: No, sir, not at all.

BIG MAN: Then just watch me and laugh when I do.

Do you know the one about the cornflakes and the Rice Krispies who had a fight?

I can only tell you a little at a time—it's a serial.

Two fleas were leaving the movie theater and one said to the other: "Shall we walk or take a dog?"

MRS. JONES: Will you join me in a cup of tea?
MRS. SMITH: I don't think there's room in there for both of us.

BETTY: That man next door has carrots growing in his ears.
HAROLD: How terrible!
BETTY: It certainly is. He planted turnips.

"Did you know that deep breathing kills germs?"
"Yes, but how do you get them to breathe deeply?"

NURSE: Well, Mr. Smith, you seem to be coughing much more easily this morning.
MR. SMITH: That's because I've been practicing all night.

"My uncle has 500 men under him."
"He must be very important."
"Not really—he's a maintenance man in a cemetery."

DENTIST: Please stop howling. I haven't even touched your tooth yet.

PATIENT: I know, but you're standing on my foot.

TEACHER: Mary, can you name four animals of the cat family?

MARY: Mother cat, father cat, and two kittens.

Advertisement in local paper:
LOST—WRISTWATCH BY A LADY WITH A CRACKED FACE

BOBBY: Dad, I'm too tired to do my homework.

DAD: Now, my boy, hard work never killed anyone yet.

BOBBY: Well, I don't want to run the risk of being the first.

TEACHER: Sidney, can you tell me how fast light travels?

SIDNEY: I don't know, but it always gets here too early in the morning.

TEACHER: Why were you absent yesterday, Tommy?

TOMMY: The doctor said I had acid indigestion.

TEACHER: Then you'd better stop drinking acid.

TEACHER: Brown, stop showing off. Do you think you're the teacher of this class?

BROWN: No, sir.

TEACHER: Right, then stop behaving like a fool.

CUSTOMER: Waiter, I've only got one piece of meat.

WAITER: Just a moment, sir, and I'll cut it in two.

Little Bernie was taking his new dog for a walk when a policeman stopped him.

"Has your dog got a license?" the policeman asked.

"Oh, no," answered Bernie. "He's not old enough to drive."

16

BARBER: Were you wearing a red
scarf when you came in?
CUSTOMER: No.
BARBER: Oh, then I must have cut
your throat.

A man came back to the dealer
from whom he bought a new car.
"I believe you gave me a
guarantee with my car," he said.
"That's right, sir," the dealer
answered. "We will replace
anything that breaks."
"Fine. I need a new garage door."

CUSTOMER: I'd like to try on that
dress in the window.
SALESLADY: I'm sorry, madam, you'll
have to use the fitting room like
everybody else.

DOCTOR: Mrs. Smith, you have acute angina.
PATIENT: I came here to be examined, not admired.

MILLY: Do you have hot water at your house?
BILLY: We sure do. And I'm always in it.

ANGRY BOSS (*to Office Boy*): You're late again this morning.
OFFICE BOY: I overslept.
ANGRY BOSS: You mean you sleep at home, *too?*

"Will the band play anything I ask them to?"
"Certainly, sir."
"Well, ask them to play chess."

FATHER: Freddie, you're a pig. Do you know what a pig is?
FREDDIE: Sure, Dad. A pig is a hog's little boy.

NURSE: Can I take your pulse?
PATIENT: Why? Haven't you got one of your own?

MOTHER LION: Son, what are you doing?
BABY LION: I am chasing a man around a tree.
MOTHER LION: How often must I tell you not to play with your food!

CUSTOMER (*in butcher's shop*): Have you got a sheep's head?
BUTCHER: No, it's just the way I part my hair.

HOTEL RECEPTIONIST IN FRANCE (*to tourist*): Are you a foreigner?
TOURIST: Certainly not! I'm from the good old U.S. of A!

"Would you like to buy a pocket calculator, sir?"
"No, thanks, I know how many pockets I've got."

19

A tourist visiting New York saw a restaurant which claimed it could supply any dish ordered, so he asked the waiter for kangaroo on toast.

After a while the waiter came back and said, "I'm so sorry, sir, but we've run out of bread."

DON: Why did Ron sleep under the oil tank last night?

JOHN: Because he wanted to get up oily in the morning.

VISITOR: Is this a healthy place to live in?

LOCAL YOKEL: Yessir, when I arrived here I couldn't walk or eat solid food.

VISITOR: What was the matter with you?

LOCAL YOKEL: Nothing—I was born here.

"The opening is for a garbage collector. Have you any experience?"

"No, but I'll pick it up as I go along."

20

2

Bad News!

SUSIE: Mother, what was the name of the last station our train stopped at?

MOTHER: I don't know—can't you see I'm reading?

SUSIE: Well, it's too bad, because that's where little Benny got off.

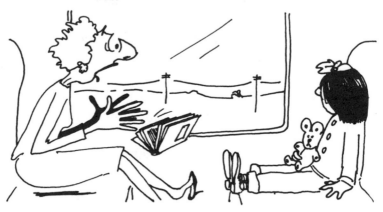

There was an Arab who was so fat—his camel had its hump underneath.

WIFE: Do you have a good
  memory for faces?
HUSBAND: Yes—why?
WIFE: I just broke your shaving
  mirror.

MOTORIST: When I bought this car you
  said it was rust-free, but the
  underneath is covered with it.
DEALER: Yes, sir. The car's rust-free.
  We didn't charge for it.

Have you heard the one about the
man who always wore sunglasses?
He took a dim view of things.

TEACHER: Bobby, can you name the
  four seasons?
BOBBY: Salt, pepper, vinegar and
  mustard.

SERGEANT (*to new recruit*): What
  were you before you joined the
  army?
NEW RECRUIT: Happy, sergeant.

HARRY: This lamb is very tough.
POLLY: I'm sorry—the butcher
  said it was spring lamb.
HARRY: Well, I must be eating
  one of the springs.

JUDGE: I don't understand why you broke into the same store three nights in a row.

PRISONER: Well, Your Honor, I picked out a dress for my wife, and I had to change it twice.

PETER: My teacher was mad because I didn't know where the pyramids were.

MOTHER (*absently*): Well, dear, next time remember where you put things.

MOVIE ATTENDANT: That's the sixth ticket you've bought.

CUSTOMER: I know—there's a girl in there that keeps tearing them up.

"My husband is so ugly that when he goes to the zoo he has to buy two tickets: one to get in and one to get out."

"This pair of shoes you sold me yesterday is ridiculous. One of them has a heel two inches shorter than the other. What am I supposed to do?"
"Limp."

TEACHER: Which is farther away—
    Australia or the moon?
BOBBY: Australia.
TEACHER: Why do you say that?
BOBBY: We can see the moon,
    and we can't see Australia.

Should you stir your tea with your left hand or your right hand?
Neither—use your spoon.

MR. JOHNSON: Are you using your mower this afternoon?
MR. SMITH: Yes.
MR. JOHNSON: Fine. Then can I borrow your tennis racket, since you won't be needing it?

SALLY: Did you see the guards change when you were in London?
LULU: No, they always pulled the blinds down.

CUSTOMER: You said this simple gadget was foolproof. I can't see how to use it.
SHOPKEEPER: Then it's what it says it is. It proves you're a fool.

"Why are you jumping up and down?"
"I've just taken some medicine and I forgot to shake the bottle."

WRITER: I took up writing full-time a year ago.
FRIEND: Have you sold anything?
WRITER: Yes—my TV, all the furniture, the house—

It's easy to make time fly. Just throw an alarm clock over your shoulder.

"I've never been troubled with backseat drivers."

"Why, what car do you drive?"

"A hearse."

A woman dashed into a hardware store and asked to be served at once.

"Give me a mousetrap, please," she gasped. "I've got to catch a train."

"I'm sorry," said the clerk. "We haven't got anything as big as that."

MOTHER: Freddie, why is your face so red?

FREDDIE: I was running up the street to stop a fight.

MOTHER: That's a very nice thing to do. Who was fighting?

FREDDIE: Me and Jackie Smith.

TEACHER: Now, Jackie, what is the highest form of animal life?

JACKIE: I think it's the giraffe.

"Why were you driving so fast?" said the policeman to the speeding motorist.

"Well, my brakes are no good, and I wanted to get home before I had an accident."

A guide was showing Niagara Falls to a man from Texas.

GUIDE: I'll bet you don't have anything like this in Texas.

TEXAN: Nope, but in Texas we have plumbers who can fix it.

How can you decide whether to use a screw or a nail when doing carpentry?

Drive in a nail—if the wood splits, you should have used a screw.

Sign in a Volkswagen factory:
THINK BIG—and you're fired.

A man was driving the wrong way down a one-way street. He was stopped by a policeman.

"This is a one-way street," said the officer.

"I know," said the motorist, "I'm only going one way."

SALESMAN: Little boy, is your mother home?

WILLIE: Yes, sir.

SALESMAN (*after knocking and knocking with no reply*): I thought you said your mother was home.

WILLIE: She is, but we don't live here.

JUDGE: Tell me, why did you park your car here?

MOTORIST: Well, there was a sign that said FINE FOR PARKING.

Due to a strike at the meteorological office, there will be no weather tomorrow.

"I went to the dentist this morning."

"Does your tooth still hurt?"

"I don't know—the dentist kept it."

"Do you write with your left hand or your right hand?"

"Neither—I write with a ballpoint pen."

A beautiful young lady kissed a prince last night—and he turned into a frog.

LADY (*on phone*): Doctor, what can I do—my little boy has swallowed my pen!

DOCTOR: Use a pencil.

A schoolboy took a book out of the library. The cover read "How to Hug." He discovered to his disappointment that it was Volume 7 of the Encyclopedia.

"My dog has no nose."
"How does it smell?"
"Terrible."

Charlie ate too many jam tarts. He clutched his stomach and groaned.
"Are you in pain?" asked his mother.
"No," moaned Charlie, "the pain's in me."

DOORMAN: Your car is at the door, sir.
CAR OWNER: Yes, I can hear it knocking.

Anybody who boasts about his ancestors is admitting that his family is better dead than alive.

WAITER: And what will you have, sir, after the steak?
DINER: Indigestion, I expect.

3

Funny Folks

"Every day my dog and I go for a tramp in the woods."

"Does the dog enjoy it?"

"Oh, yes—but the tramp is a bit fed up."

"I hear you've fallen in love with Dracula."

"Yes, it was love at first bite."

"He's so wealthy, he bought a boy for his dogs to play with."

MOTHER: Now, Monty, you know you're not supposed to eat with your knife.
MONTY: I know, Ma, but my fork leaks.

BETTY: I had a fall last night which left me unconscious for eight hours.
HETTY: How dreadful! Where did you fall?
BETTY: I fell asleep.

CUSTOMER: I'd like two pork chops, please, and make them lean.
BUTCHER: Yes, madam, which way?

YOUNG MAN: Er, excuse me—but would you go out with me tonight?
DOLLY: Oh, I don't go out with perfect strangers.
YOUNG MAN: I never said I was perfect!

One egg boiling in a pot said to another egg in the pot: "Gosh, it's hot in here."

Said the other egg: "Wait till you get out and have your head bashed in!"

PATIENT: Will my measles be better next week, doctor?

DOCTOR: I don't like to make rash promises.

CUSTOMER (*to Bank Manager*): Will you help me out, please?

BANK MANAGER: Certainly—go through that door.

OLD MAN (*to his wife*): What on earth are you doing?

WIFE: Knitting up some barbed-wire fence.

OLD MAN: How can you do that?

WIFE: I'm using steel wool.

"Will you kiss me?"

"But I have scruples."

"That's all right—I've been vaccinated."

TEACHER: I wish you'd pay a little attention.

ANGIE: I'm paying as little as I can.

After the dance, the young man asked the young lady if he could see her home—so she showed him a photograph of it.

BERT: Mom, there's a man with a bill at the door.
MOMMY: Don't be silly, dear, it must be a duck with a hat on.

BRIGHT BILLY: Dad, is your watch going?
DAD: Yes, of course it is.
BRIGHT BILLY: Then when's it coming back?

MAN (*on telephone to Weather Bureau*): What are the chances of a shower today?
WEATHERMAN: It's okay with me, sir. If you want one, take one.

PATIENT: What can you give me
for flat feet, Doctor?
DOCTOR: Have you tried a bicycle
pump?

GUIDE (*on safari*): Quick, sir, shoot
that leopard right on the spot.
LORD CLARENCE: Be specific, man,
which spot?

LADY: Waiter, please bring me coffee
without cream.
WAITER: I'm afraid we've run out of
cream. Would you like it without
milk?

Notice in a pet shop: IN THE
INTEREST OF DOGS, HYGIENE IS
NOT PERMITTED IN THIS SHOP.

The more we study, the more we know.
The more we know, the more we forget.
The more we forget, the less we know.
So, why study?

The fat lady walked into the dress shop. "I'd like to see a dress that would fit me," she told the clerk.

"So would I," said the tactless clerk.

HARRY: Have you read the Bible?
SALLY: No, I'm waiting for the film.

Willy came home from Sunday School and asked his mother, "Do people really come from dust?"

"In a way," said his mother.

"And do they go back to dust?"

"Yes, in a way."

"Well, mother, I looked under my bed, and somebody's either coming or going."

CUSTOMER: Why is this chop so very tough?
WAITER: Well, sir, it's a karate chop.

One day a worried-looking man knocked at a lady's door. "I'm very sorry, lady," he said, "I've just run over your cat and I'd like to replace it."

"Well," said the lady doubtfully, "can you catch mice?"

PATIENT: I still feel very tired, doctor.
DOCTOR: Didn't you take those sleeping pills I gave you?
PATIENT: Well, they looked so peaceful in the little bottle that I didn't like to wake them up.

A farmer had a large hay field. His son didn't want to stay on the farm, so he moved to town; but the only job he could get was shining shoes, so now the farmer makes hay while the son shines.

"My mother gave Dad some soap flakes instead of cornflakes for his breakfast, by mistake."

"Was he mad?"

"He certainly was. He foamed at the mouth."

"My husband is very religious— he won't work if there's a Sunday in the week."

CECIL: Do you know how many days belong to the year?

CLAUD: All of them, I suppose.

CECIL: Nope, just 325. The rest are Lent.

1ST CANNIBAL: I feel sick every time I eat a missionary.

2ND CANNIBAL: That's because you can't keep a good man down.

4

Surprise!

What were Tarzan's last words?
Who greased the vine?

The old lady was being interviewed by the press after she had reached the age of 110. "What do you think is the reason for your long life?" they asked her.

She thought for a while. "Well," she said, "I suppose it's because I was born such a long time ago."

SID: My father can play the piano by ear.

DON: That's nothing—my father fiddles with his whiskers.

FATHER: Don't go into the water right after lunch. It's dangerous to swim on a full stomach.

SON: That's all right, Dad, I'll swim on my back.

Two children were watching a motorboat pull a man on skis across a lake. "What makes that boat go so fast?" asked little Lucy.

"It's because that man on the string is chasing it," said her brother.

MOTHER: Didn't I tell you to let me know when the soup began to boil?

JOE: Yes, and I'm telling you. It was half past one.

TIM: Mother, you'd better come out. I've just knocked over the ladder at the side of the house.
MOTHER: I'm busy—run and tell your father.
TIM: He already knows. He's hanging from the roof.

MR. BROWN: I've noticed Mr. Johnson's manners have improved lately.
MRS. BROWN: Yes, he got a job in a refinery.

STARTER (*at boat race*): Come in, Number 9—your time is up.
ASSISTANT: But we've only got eight boats.
STARTER: Are you in trouble, Number 6?

"I was an unwanted child—my mother wanted puppies."

In Dodge City the Sheriff arrested
Lulu Belle for wearing a taffeta dress.
"What's the charge, Sheriff?" she
asked.
"Rustlin', of course," he replied.

DAN: When I grow up, I'm going to
be a policeman and follow in my
father's footprints.
STAN: I didn't know your father was a
policeman.
DAN: He's not—he's a burglar.

TOMMY: Are worms good to eat?
DAD: I shouldn't think so. Why?
TOMMY: There was one in your pie.

Why do cows in Switzerland have
bells around their necks?
Because their horns don't work.

Goofy Gus went into a shop with a mince pie stuck in each ear.

"Excuse me," said the salesclerk, "but you've got mince pies in your ears."

"You'll have to speak up," said Goofy Gus. "I've got mince pies in my ears."

POSTMAN: I have a parcel here, but the name on it is obliterated.
JACKSON: Can't be for me, then. My name's Jackson.

The poet had been droning on at the party about his various sources of inspiration. "Yes," he told the young girl, "I'm at present collecting some of my better poems to be published posthumously."

"Lovely," said the girl. "I'll look forward to it."

Harry and Larry were given a toboggan for Christmas. After they had been out playing in the snow, Larry was in tears.

"Now, Harry," said his father, "I told you to let Larry use the toboggan half the time."

"And I did," said Harry, "I had it going down, and he had it going up."

"Is your new horse well-behaved?"

"Oh, yes. When we come to a fence, he stops and lets me go over first."

HUSBAND: What would you like for your birthday?

WIFE: Oh—let it be a surprise.

HUSBAND: Right . . . BOO!

JILL: Daddy, Jack's broken my new doll.

DADDY: How did he do that?

JILL: I hit him on the head with it.

Little Caroline was drawing a Nativity picture—there were Mary and Joseph, shepherds and wise men.

"What's that in the corner?" asked her teacher.

"That's their TV, of course," replied Caroline.

A woman was driving the wrong way down a one-way street and was stopped by a policeman.

"Didn't you see the arrows?" he asked.

"Arrows? I didn't even see the Indians," she said.

Dolphins are so intelligent that within a few weeks of captivity they can train a man to stand on the edge of their pool and throw them fish three times a day.

MOTHER: Did you behave well in church today, Margie?

MARGIE: I certainly did. A nice man offered me a plate full of money, and I said, "No, thank you."

Pedestrian: a person who can be easily reached by car.

TEACHER: Now, Brenda, how many fingers have you?

BRENDA: Ten.

TEACHER: Right. Now if you lost four of them in an accident, what would you have?

BRENDA: No more piano lessons.

FRIEND: And what are you going to give your baby brother for his birthday, Janet?

JANET: I don't know—last year I gave him measles.

A policeman saw an old man pulling a box on a leash down a busy street. "Poor man," he thought. "I'd better humor him."

"That's a nice dog you've got there," he said to the old man.

"It isn't a dog, it's a box," said the old man.

"Oh, I'm sorry," said the policeman, "I thought you were a bit simpleminded," and he walked on.

The old man turned and looked at the box. "We fooled him that time, Rover," he said.

46

Young Tim was raking leaves with his father who was telling him about how the fairies turned the leaves brown. He looked up pityingly at his father. "Haven't you ever heard of photosynthesis?" he asked.

BROWN: I cured my son of biting his nails.
GREEN: Oh, how did you manage that?
BROWN: I knocked all his teeth out.

What does 36 inches make in Glasgow?
One Scotland Yard.

The visitor stared in amazement at the child knocking nails into the posh Scandinavian furniture.

He turned to his host. "Don't you find it expensive to let your son play games like that?" he asked.

"Not really," replied the host. "I get the nails wholesale."

POLICEMAN: I'm sorry, Sonny, but you need a permit to fish here.
SONNY: That's all right, thanks. I'm doing okay with a worm.

NEW HUSBAND: Just think, darling—
we've now been married for
twenty-four hours!
NEW WIFE: Yes, darling, and it seems
like only yesterday.

GORDON: How's your sister
doing with her reducing diet?
CHARLIE: Fine—she disappeared
last week.

MORRIS: Can you spell blind pig?
NORMAN: B-l-i-n-d p-i-g.
MORRIS: No. It's b-l-n-d p-g. With
two i's, he wouldn't be blind.

Sign in a Police Station: IT
TAKES ABOUT 3500 BOLTS
TO PUT A CAR TOGETHER
BUT ONLY ONE NUT TO
SCATTER IT ALL OVER
THE ROAD.

5

Excuse Me!

A very fat lady sitting on the bus noticed three elderly ladies standing. Turning to the man next to her, she said, "If you were a gentleman, you'd get up and let one of those ladies sit down."

"If you were a lady," he replied, "you'd get up and let all three of them sit down."

MOTHER: Why is your little brother crying?

BILLY: Because I won't give him my piece of cake.

MOTHER: Is his piece gone?

BILLY: Yes—he cried when I ate that, too.

Goofy Gus took a friend driving on a narrow mountain road. After a while the friend said, "I feel very scared whenever you go around one of those sharp bends."

"Then do what I do," said Gus, "close your eyes."

"Our next comedian is so bad that when he took part in an outdoor show in the park, twenty-six trees got up and walked out."

FATHER (*at breakfast*): My goodness, son, that was some thunderstorm we had last night.

SON: It certainly was.

MOTHER: Oh, dear, why didn't you wake me up? You know I can't sleep in a thunderstorm.

CUSTOMER: Those sausages you sent me were meat at one end and bread at the other.

BUTCHER: Yes, madam, in these times, it's difficult to make both ends meat.

LADY: I found a fly in one of those currant buns you sold me yesterday.

SHOP OWNER: Well, bring it back and I'll exchange it for a currant.

MAN (*to psychiatrist*): I'm worried—I keep thinking I'm a pair of curtains.

PSYCHIATRIST: Stop worrying and pull yourself together.

DOCTOR (*after listening to his patient's numerous complaints*): I'll write something out for you.

PATIENT: Is it a prescription?

DOCTOR: No, it's a letter of introduction to the undertaker.

51

One day Mr. Jones came home to find his wife wringing her hands and weeping. "Oh, dear," she said, "the cat's eaten your dinner."

"Never mind," he said. "We can get a new cat tomorrow."

Simple Simon went to buy a pillow case.

"What size?" said the clerk.

"I don't know," said Simon. "But I wear a seven-and-a-half hat."

JINKS: I notice your neighbor doesn't let his chickens run loose any more. Why is that?

BINKS: Well, I hid six eggs under a bush the other night. Next day I made sure he saw me collect the eggs.

A young lady went into a bank to withdraw some money.

"Can you identify yourself?" asked the clerk.

The young lady opened her handbag, took out a mirror, looked into it and said, "Yes, it's me, all right."

PIANO TUNER: I've come to tune your piano.

LADY: But we didn't send for you.

PIANO TUNER: No, but your neighbors did.

YOUNG MAN: I've come to ask for your daughter's hand.

FATHER: You'll have to take all of her or it's no deal.

The medical lecturer turned to one of his students and said, "Now, Merryweather, it is clear from this X-ray that one of this patient's legs is much shorter than the other. This accounts for the patient's limp. But what would *you* do in a case like this?"

Merryweather thought for a moment, then said brightly, "Well, sir, I should imagine that I would limp, too."

Sammy had been on an outing with his father.

"Well," said his mother, when they got home, "did you like the zoo?"

"Oh, it was fine," replied Sammy. "And Dad liked it, too—especially when one of the animals came romping home at 20 to 1."

News broadcast: Two prisoners escaped today from Wakefield prison. One is seven feet tall and the other is four feet six. The police are hunting high and low for them.

BROWN: The police are looking for a man with one eye called Smith.
WHITE: What's his other eye called?

CLOAKROOM ATTENDANT: Please leave your hat here, sir.

CLUB CUSTOMER: I haven't got a hat.

ATTENDANT: Then I'm afraid you can't come into the club. My orders are that people cannot enter unless they leave their hats in the cloakroom.

A lady decided to breed chickens, but she didn't have much luck. At last, she wrote to the Department of Agriculture for some advice. She wrote: "Dear Sir, Every morning I find one or two of my prize chickens lying stiff and cold on the ground with their legs in the air. Would you kindly tell me what is the matter?"

A few days later she got this reply: "Dear Madam, Your chickens are dead."

BARRY: How many balls of string would it take to reach the moon?

LARRY: Only one—if it were long enough.

GREEDY BOY: I got through a jar of jam today.

FRIEND: It must have been a tight squeeze.

ONE BIRD (*to his friend*): Look, there's a Concorde. I wish I could go as fast as that.

FRIEND BIRD: You could, if your bottom was on fire.

The pilot felt a gun sticking in his back, and a voice hissed in his ear, "Take me to London."

"But we're going to London," said the pilot.

"I know. But I've been hijacked to Cuba twice before, so this time I'm taking no chances."

POLLY: What's the weather like?

MOLLY: I don't know—it's so cloudy I can't see.

GRANDMA: I like to go to bed and get up with the chickens, don't you?

BETTY: No, I like to sleep in my own bed.

NED: What goes ninety-nine bump, ninety-nine bump, ninety-nine bump?

ED: A centipede with a wooden leg.

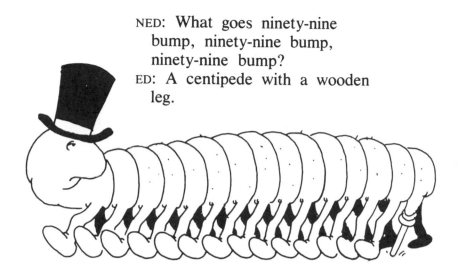

OLD SALT: I once had a parrot for five years and it never said a word.

YOUNG SAILOR: It must have been tongue-tied.

OLD SALT: No, it was stuffed.

MOLLY: Did you hear the one about the bed?

POLLY: No.

MOLLY: It hasn't been made up yet.

"Why are you drinking blue and white paint?"

"Because I'm an interior decorator."

ROGER: Your overcoat is very loud.

RODNEY: It's not so bad when I put on a muffler.

JUDGE: I shall give you a short
sentence.
PRISONER: Thank you, Your Honor.
JUDGE: Ten years.
PRISONER: Ten years—that's not a
short sentence!
JUDGE: Yes, it is—two words.

A man bought a grandfather clock
from an antique shop. In the street
he put it over his shoulder, and as he
did so, knocked over an old lady.
"Idiot," she yelled, "why can't you
wear a wristwatch like the rest of
us?"

"Waiter, there's a button in my
salad."
"Oh, it must have come off when
the salad was dressing."

"Why did Lulu leave her job?"
"Illness."
"Anything serious?"
"Yes. The boss got sick of her."

PATIENT: If I take these little blue pills, as you suggest, will I get better?
DOCTOR: Well, put it this way— none of my patients has ever come back to ask for more.

"Doctor, I feel like a pack of cards."
"Wait over there, I'll deal with you later."

WAITER: We have practically everything on the menu.
DINER: So I see—would you bring me a clean one, please?

A visitor was being shown around a farm, when he saw a bull in a field. He called out, "Is that bull safe?"
"Well," said the farmer, "offhand I'd say he's a lot safer than you are."

FRED: What is the noblest dog?
NED: The hot dog—it feeds the hand that bites it.

After robbing the bank, the thief rushed home and began to saw the legs off his bed. His wife asked him what he was doing.

"I want to lie low for a while," he explained.

HETTY: My doctor put me on a diet, using more corn and vegetable oils.
BETTY: Does it work?
HETTY: I don't know yet. I'm not thinner, but I don't squeak any more.

MOTHER: Willy, it's rude to keep stretching across the table for the cake. Haven't you got a tongue?
WILLY: Yes, but my arm's longer.

OFFICE MANAGER: Look at all the dust on this desk. It looks as if it hasn't been cleaned for a month and a half.
CLEANING LADY: Don't blame me, sir, I've only been here a week.

6

How Odd . . .

Three rather deaf old friends met one day.

"Windy, isn't it?" said one.

"No, it's Thursday," said the second.

"So am I," said the third. "Let's go and have a cup of tea."

1ST PATIENT: I see they've brought in another case of tonsillitis.

2ND PATIENT: Anything is better than that lousy lemonade they've been giving us lately.

WRITER: Do you know it took me over twenty years to find out I have no writing ability.

ACQUAINTANCE: So what did you do—give it up?

WRITER: Oh, no, by then I was so famous I couldn't afford to.

Newton discovered gravity when an apple hit him on the head. He was shaken to the core.

LADY (*dialing 911*): Help! Please come to my house at once!

POLICEMAN: What's the trouble, lady?

LADY: That dreadful new postman is sitting up in a tree in my front yard, teasing my dog.

NEW BRIDEGROOM: Darling, do you think you'll be able to put up with my ugly mug for the rest of your life?

BRIDE: I expect so, dear, you'll be out at work all day.

MAN: My dog has no tail.

FRIEND: Then how do you know when he's happy?

MAN: Oh, he stops biting me.

BEN: I hear the workers are striking for shorter hours.

LEN: Good thing, too—I always did think sixty minutes was too long for an hour.

HUSBAND: I've just discovered oil.

WIFE: Wonderful. Now we can get a new car.

HUSBAND: We'd better get the old one fixed first—that's where the oil's coming from.

JUDGE: As the jury has found you Not Guilty of fraud, you are now free to go.

PRISONER: Does that mean I can keep the money?

After class, the absentminded professor asked if anybody had seen his coat.

"You have it on, sir," he was told.

"Oh, thank you very much," he replied. "Otherwise, I might have gone off without it."

Silly Billy came home from the railway station complaining that he felt ill because he had been riding backwards for three hours on the train.

"Why didn't you ask the person sitting opposite you to change seats?" his mother asked.

"I couldn't," he said. "There wasn't anybody sitting opposite me."

A little boy noticed some green parakeets in a pet shop.

"Look, Mommy," he said, "there are some canaries that aren't ripe."

ROGER: My girl friend and I had a row the other night— she wanted to go to the ballet, and I wanted to go to a pop concert. But we came to an agreement.

PETER: What ballet did you see?

RICK: I just got a bottle of vodka for my mother-in-law.
VIC: Sounds like a good swap.

BILL: Do you have holes in your trousers?
JIM: Certainly not.
BILL: Then how do you get your legs through?

LADY (*visiting artist in his studio*): Do you like painting people in the nude?
ARTIST: No, personally I prefer painting with my clothes on.

MIKE: Does your wife cook by gas or electricity?
JAKE: I don't know, I've never tried to cook her.

FRANK: Four sailors fell in the sea,
but only one of them got his hair
wet.
JOHNNY: How was that?
FRANK: Three of them were bald.

VISITOR (*at gate*): Does your
dog bite strangers?
MAN: Only when he doesn't
know them.

The professor was checking papers
in his study when his telephone rang.
His secretary answered it. "Long
distance from New York," she said.
"Yes, I know," answered the
professor.

Dying words of a famous
Chicago gangster: "Who put
that violin in my violin case?"

TEACHER: Now can somebody tell me where elephants are found?

MARY: Well, elephants are so big they are hardly ever lost.

MRS. GREEN: I see you and your husband are taking French lessons—why is that?

MRS. BLACK: We've adopted a French baby, and we want to be able to understand him as soon as he learns to talk.

The professor looked at one of his students. "Haven't you a brother who took this course last year?" he asked.

"No, sir," said the student. "I'm just taking it again."

"My word," said the professor, "amazing resemblance."

What did the penny say when it got stuck in the slot?

"Money's very tight these days."

RON: You dance beautifully.

JEAN: I wish I could say the same for you.

RON: You could—if you were as big a liar as I am.

TEACHER (*on phone*): You say Tommy has a cold and can't come to school? To whom am I speaking?
VOICE: This is my father.

ADAM: And I shall call that creature over there a rhinoceros.
EVE: But why call it that?
ADAM: Because it looks like a rhinoceros, stupid.

If at first you don't succeed, you're just like 99.9 percent of the population.

JACKIE: I wouldn't marry you if you were the last person on earth.
JOHNNY: If I were, you wouldn't be here.

VISITOR: And how do you like going to school, Willie?

WILLIE: I like going, and I like coming back. It's the bit in between I don't like.

WAITER: Yes, sir, you can have anything you see on the menu.

DINER: Well, how about dirty fingermarks, grease stains, and gravy—in that order.

LARGE LADY: I'm very annoyed with that scale.

FRIEND: Why's that?

LARGE LADY: When I stepped on it, it said, "One person at a time, please."

 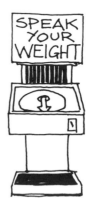

How do we know that Moses wore a wig?

Because sometimes he was seen with Aaron and sometimes without.

TAD: How do fishermen make their nets, Dad?

DAD: Easily. They just take a lot of holes and sew them together.

Wholesome—the only thing from which you can take the whole and still have some left.

Sarah hadn't been paying attention when the teacher was explaining the importance of milk. When the teacher asked her to name six things with milk in them, she thought for a moment. Then she said, "Hot chocolate, ice cream, rice pudding—and three cows."

"My mother-in-law has gone to Indonesia."

"Jakarta?"

"No—she went by plane."

7

Oh, No!

Two little boys were looking at an abstract painting in an art shop.

"Let's run," said one, "before they say we did it."

MUGGER: Will you give me your money or shall I shoot you?

BURT: Shoot me. I need the money for my old age.

"Your money or your life," said the mugger to the miser. When there was no reply, he repeated the demand. "Come on, man, your money or your life, which will it be?"

"Quiet," said the miser, "I'm thinking about it."

WALTER: A steamroller ran over my uncle.
RICHARD: What did you do?
WALTER: I took him home and slipped him under the door.

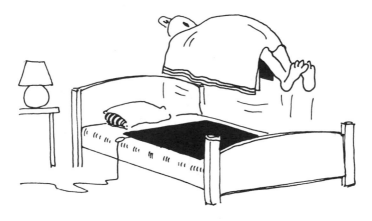

PAT: I didn't sleep well last night.
MATT: Why was that?
PAT: I plugged the electric blanket into the toaster by mistake and kept popping out of bed all night.

SUZIE: I'd like two ounces of bird seed, please.

PET SHOP OWNER: How many birds have you, dear?

SUZIE: None right now, but I want to grow some.

A lady went to buy some wool to knit a sweater for her dog.

"Perhaps you'd better bring him in," said the saleslady. "Then I can tell you how much wool to buy."

"Oh, no," said the customer, "it's supposed to be a surprise!"

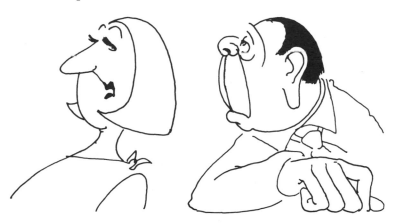

"Darling, you have the face of a saint."
"Thank you, darling, which saint?"
"A Saint Bernard."

LADY: Can this wool coat be worn in wet weather?

CLERK: Madam, have you ever seen a sheep carry an umbrella?

A man came to the police station and complained, "I've got three brothers—we all live in one room. One of my brothers has six cats; another has five dogs, and the other has a goat. The smell is terrible. Can you do something about it?"

"Well, why don't you open the windows?" asked the policeman.

"What? And lose all my pigeons?"

PROUD MOTHER: My baby is a year old now, and he's been walking since he was eight months old.

BORED VISITOR: Really? He must be awfully tired.

Father was showing Tommy the family album, and came across a picture of himself and his wife on their wedding day.

"Was that the day Mommy came to work for us?" Tommy asked.

Percival was so wealthy that even
the bags under his eyes had his
initials on them.

"Doctor, you remember last year
you told me to stay away from
dampness if I wanted my rheumatism
to get better?"
"Yes," said the doctor.
"Well, it's better. Is it all right for
me to take a bath now?"

The mother kangaroo leaped into
the air with a cry of pain.
"Joey," she said, "how many times
do I have to tell you not to smoke
in bed!"

A beginning rider at the stables was trying to saddle a horse.

"Excuse me," said the old hand, "but you're putting that saddle on backwards."

"How do you know," snapped the beginner. "You don't know which way I'm going."

Keep smiling—it makes everyone wonder what you're up to.

TOURIST: Whose skull is that?

TIRED GUIDE: That, sir, is the skull of Julius Caesar.

TOURIST: Then whose is that small one beside it?

GUIDE: That, sir, is the skull of Julius Caesar when he was a small boy.

JACK: What did the bald man say when he received a comb for his birthday?

TOM: I don't know, what did he say?

JACK: Thanks very much, I'll never part with it.

The census taker knocked on Miss Matty's door. She answered all his questions except one. She refused to tell him her age.

"But everybody tells their age to the census taker," he said.

"Did Miss Maisie Hill and Miss Daisy Hill tell you their ages?"

"Certainly."

"Well, I'm the same age as they are," she snapped.

"As old as the Hills," he wrote on his form.

POST OFFICE CLERK: Here's your twenty-cent stamp.

SHOPPER (*with arms full of packages*): Do I have to stick it on myself?

POST OFFICE CLERK: No, on the envelope.

LITTLE GIRL: I was going to buy you some hankies for Christmas, Uncle, but I couldn't remember the size of your nose.

Young Larry and Barry were watching men on high scaffolding, repairing a tall chimney.

"What would you do if you were up there and that thing fell?" Larry asked.

"I would wait until it got nearly to the ground and then I would jump."

> HUSBAND (*phoning his wife from his office*): I've got two tickets for the ballet.
> WIFE: Oh, lovely, I'll start getting ready.
> HUSBAND: Yes, do—the tickets are for tomorrow night.

8

Give & Take

"Excuse me, can you tell me the time?"

"I'm sorry—I'm a stranger here myself."

TEACHER: What is a skeleton?
MARVIN: It's a man with his outsides off and his insides out.

It was the old missionaries in Africa who gave the cannibals their first taste of Christianity.

TEACHER: I hope I didn't see you looking at someone else's paper, Jamie.

JAMIE: I hope so too, teacher.

"My uncle gets a warm reception wherever he goes."
"He must be very popular."
"No, he's a fireman."

Bert had a letter from his mother. "Dear Bert, so much has happened since you were home. I've had all my teeth out, and a new gas stove put in. . . ."

What happened to the cat who swallowed a ball of wool?
She had mittens.

Harvey received a letter from his wife:
"Dear Harvey, I missed you yesterday. Please come home again and let me have another shot."

WILLIE: What is frozen tea?
SAMMY: Iced tea.
WILLY: What is frozen beer?
SAMMY: Iced beer.
WILLY: What is frozen ink?
SAMMY: Iced ink.
WILLY: Well, go and have a bath.

DAN: This match won't light.
STAN: Why, what's the matter with it?
DAN: I don't know—it was all right a minute ago.

"I've made the chicken soup."
"Good—I was afraid it was for us."

MORRIS: I hear the workers in the mint are complaining about having too much work to do.

HARRIS: Yes, they're threatening to go out on strike unless they make less money.

FATHER: I'm worried about you always being at the bottom of your class.

FREDDIE: Don't worry, Dad. They teach the same thing at both ends.

"Where did I come from?" asked the baby ear of corn.

"The stalk brought you," answered its mother.

"I understand you buried your husband last week?"

"Yes—I had to: he was dead."

82

PRETTY GIRL (*at party to best-selling author*): Oh, I've read all your books—the one I liked best was the one with the green leather cover and the gold lettering—

Overheard at Magicians' Convention: "Hi, there, Terry, how's tricks?"

SMITH: You seem to have been working in your garden. Mr. Brown— what are you growing?
BROWN: Tired.

When Buster was born they fired twenty-one guns. Unfortunately they all missed.

SMUG CITIZEN: You should pay your taxes with a smile.
FRIEND: Yes, I'd like to, but they insist on cash.

DOCTOR: How are you now, Mr. Gibson, after your heart operation?
MR. GIBSON: Well, Doctor, I'm fine, but I seem to have two heartbeats.
DOCTOR: Oh, dear, I wondered where my wristwatch had gone.

MO: Where do you weigh whales?
JO: I don't know.
MO: At a whale weigh station, of
course!

MOTHER: Eat your cabbage, dear, it
will put color into your cheeks.
ANGIE: Who wants green cheeks?

"You can't help admiring our boss."
"Why is that?"
"If you don't—you're fired."

The lady with the large flowery hat
was stopped at the church door by
the usher. "Are you a friend of the
bride?" he asked.
"Certainly not," she snapped. "I'm
the bridegroom's mother."

"I think grandma needs new glasses."

"What makes you say that, son?"

"She's been watching two pairs of father's trousers going around in the washing machine—and thinks she's watching a wrestling match on TV."

HENRY: This old tramp came up to me and said he hadn't had a bite in two weeks.

BOB: Poor fellow—what did you do?

HENRY: Bit him, of course!

OFFICE MANAGER: I'm afraid that young man I hired isn't honest.

ACCOUNTS CLERK: Oh, you shouldn't judge by appearance.

OFFICE MANAGER: I'm not—I'm judging by disappearance!

GEORGE: I see you're still on crutches, old man.

LEON: Yes—that's the last time I'll try and jump over the net at table tennis.

"What's a girl like you doing in a nice place like this?"

BARBER (*to youth with slick plastered-down hair*): Do you just want me to cut it or would you like an oil check, too?

MRS. WHITE: Where are you living now, Mrs. Green?

MRS. GREEN: Just by the river—drop in some time.

"Oh, Doctor, I swallowed the film out of my camera!"

"Well, we'll just have to hope that nothing develops."

SALESMAN: Would you like to try our new oatmeal soap?

LADY: No, thank you, I never wash my oatmeal.

SIMON: Which side of the bed do you sleep on?

DOPEY DAN: The top side, of course.

DOUG: What do you think happened
to the plant in our arithmetic class?
DICK: I don't know, what?
DOUG: It grew square roots.

TAILOR: Your suit will be ready in two
months, sir.
CUSTOMER: Two months! It only took
six days when God made the
world.
TAILOR: True, sir, but look at the state
the world is in.

MAUD: Samantha reminds me of
a film star.
IVY: Really—which one?
MAUD: Lassie.

VOICE (*on phone*): Is Mr. Miller in
yet?
SECRETARY: No, he hasn't even been
in yesterday yet.

THIEF: Quick—the police are coming—jump out of the window!

ACCOMPLICE: But we're on the thirteenth floor!

THIEF: This is no time to be superstitious.

"Waiter, this coffee tastes like mud."

"Well, sir, it was ground only five minutes ago."

"How did you get the flat tire?"

"Ran over a milk bottle."

"But didn't you see it?"

"No—the kid had it hidden under his coat."

"I think I've got measles."

"That's a rash thing to say."

"Why don't you answer the telephone?"

"It's not ringing."

"Oh, you always have to leave everything till the last minute."

The muddled old gentleman went up to another man at the conference. "I hardly recognized you," he said. "You've changed so much: your hair is different, you seem shorter, you've done away with your glasses. What's happened to you, Mr. Frost?"

"But I'm not Mr. Frost."

"Amazing—you've even changed your name!"

"And how do you like the meatballs?"

"I don't know—I've never been to any."

Little Diana was standing in front of her mirror with her eyes closed.

"Why are you standing there with your eyes closed?" asked her brother.

"So I can see what I look like when I'm asleep," she replied.

PATIENT: I always feel that I'm covered in gold paint, Doctor.
PSYCHIATRIST: Oh, that's just your gilt complex.

JULIE: That boy's annoying me.
WENDY: Why, he's not even looking at you.
JULIE: I know, that's what's annoying me.

CLARE: I see you're invited to Sandra's party.
ZELDA: Yes, but I can't go. The invitation says 4 to 7, and I'm eight.

FATHER: What's that gash on your forehead?
SILLY SON: I bit myself.
FATHER: How on earth could you do that?
SILLY SON: I stood on a chair.

TEACHER: Wendy, say a sentence beginning with 'I.'
WENDY: "I is . . ."
TEACHER: No, Wendy, you must say, "I *am*."
WENDY: All right, I *am* the ninth letter of the alphabet.

TEACHER: You know that Russell boy?
PRINCIPAL: What about him?
TEACHER: Not only is he the worst-behaved child in the school, but he has a perfect attendance record.

90

9

Show & Tell

A lady went to visit a friend and carried a small box with holes punched in the top.

"What's in your box?" asked the friend.

"A cat," said the lady. "You see I've been dreaming about mice at night and I'm so scared! This cat is to catch them."

"But the mice are only imaginary," said the friend.

"So is the cat," whispered the lady.

MAN (*in restaurant*): Excuse me,
waiter, how long have you been
working here?
WAITER: About two months, sir.
MAN: Oh, then it couldn't have been
you who took my order.

I stayed on a farm and one day a
chicken died, so we had roast
chicken. The next day a pig died and
we had pork chops. The following
day the farmer died—so I left.

ERIC: I've been asked to get married
hundreds of times.
GLORIA (*surprised*): By whom?
ERIC: My parents.

"Do you sell dog's meat?"
"Only if they come in with their
owners."

92

MOTHER: Shall I put the kettle on?
FATHER: No, dear, I don't think it would suit you.

MOLLY: That's a nice suit you're wearing.
HARRY: Oh, do you like it?
MOLLY: Yes, who went for the fitting?

RECEPTIONIST: Doctor Chaunchadinjhi is waiting for you, sir.
PATIENT: Which doctor?
RECEPTIONIST: Oh, no, he's fully qualified.

STUDENT: Did you say you learned to play the violin in six easy lessons?
MASTER: That's right. It was the seven hundred that came afterwards that were the hard ones.

GIRL (*standing in the middle of a busy road*): Officer, can you tell me the fastest way to get to the hospital?
POLICEMAN: Just stay right where you are.

RUPERT: How many dead people are there in a cemetery?
ROBERT: All of them.

"Charlie," called out the news editor to his cub reporter, "did you get that story about the man who sings tenor and baritone at the same time?"

"There's no story, sir," said the reporter. "The man has two heads."

YOUNG FISHERMAN: Is this a good river for fish?

OLD FISHERMAN: It must be—I can't get any of them to come out.

Two ladies met after a long time.

MRS. HUGHES: I believe your son is a very good football player. What position does he play?

MRS. EVANS: Oh, I believe he's one of the drawbacks.

LITTLE DIANA: Can you stand on your head?

LULU: No, I can't get my feet up high enough.

VIC: I've changed my mind.

DICK: Thank goodness. Does the new one work any better?

LESLIE: Did your mother go in for weight lifting?

WESLEY: No, why?

LESLIE: Well, how did she ever raise a dumbbell like you?

MAYOR (*to Visitor*): What do you think of our town band?

VISITOR: I think it ought to be.

MAYOR (*puzzled*): Ought to be what?

VISITOR: Banned.

A large hole was discovered in the walls surrounding the Carefree Nudist Camp. The police are looking into it.

The income tax expert was visiting the school to talk about taxes. "I'm going to tell you now about *indirect* taxes. Can anybody tell me what an indirect tax is?"

"A dog license," said Smart Alec.

"Why is that?" asked the expert.

"The dog doesn't pay it."

AUNTIE: Well, Billy, how do you like school?

BILLY: Closed.

VIC: She sure gave you a dirty look.

DICK: Who?

VIC: Mother Nature!

"Did you hear the one about the piece of rope?"
"No."
"Aw, skip it."

PATIENT: Doctor, do you think lemons are healthy?
DOCTOR: Well, I've never heard one complain.

ROSIE: This ointment makes my leg smart.
ROB: Well, why not rub some on your head!

BERNIE: Dad, would you do my arithmetic for me?
DAD: No, son, it wouldn't be right.
BERNIE: Well, at least you could try.

Mr. Briggs was making a knotty pine bookcase. His young son pointed to it and said, "What are those holes for?"

"They're *knot* holes," replied his father.

"Well," said the lad, "if they're not holes, what are they?"

MOTHER: Where are you off to, Hubert?

HUBERT: I'm going to watch a solar eclipse.

MOTHER: All right, dear, but don't get too close.

PRISON OFFICER: Sir, I have to report that ten prisoners have broken out.

WARDEN: Blow the whistles, sound the alarms, alert the police—

PRISON OFFICER: Shouldn't we call the doctor first—it looks as if it might be measles.

OFFICE MANAGER: How well can you type?

DAN: Oh, not very well, but I can rub out at sixty-five words a minute.

The office manager looked towards his secretary who was absorbed in painting her fingernails.

"Miss Bright," he said, "I'd like to compliment you on your work—but when are you going to do any?"

Tim at boarding school, sent this telegram to his father asking for money: "No mon, no fun, your son."

Back came the reply: "How sad, too bad, your dad."

RONALD: My wife's a kleptomaniac.

DONALD: Is she taking anything for it?

DWAYNE: Mommy, why do you have so much gray hair?

MOMMY: I expect it's because you are so naughty and cause me so much worry.

DWAYNE: Oh—you must have been terrible to Grandma!

LADY CUSTOMER: I'd like a shirt for my husband.

CLERK: Yes, madam, what size?

LADY CUSTOMER: I don't know, but I can just get both my hands around his neck, if that's any help.

After the telephone was installed in her home, the lady called the operator.

"My telephone cord is too long," she said. "Would you please pull it a little from your end?"

PAM: You see, Doctor, I'm always dizzy for half an hour after I get up in the morning.

DOCTOR: Well, try getting up half an hour later.

WORRIED LADY PASSENGER: Captain, do ships this size sink very often?

CAPTAIN: No, madam, never more than once.

In the attic Gloria found an old family Bible. When she opened it, a large pressed leaf fell out.

"Aha!" she said, "Adam must have left his clothes here."

STEVE: How did you get that black eye?

STAN: I got hit by a guided muscle.

TEACHER: Sammy, what is water?
SAMMY: Water is a colorless liquid that turns black when I put my hands in it.

AUNTIE MAY: Well, Susan, what are you going to do when you're as big as your mother?
SUSAN: Go on a diet.

REGGIE: I'm going to buy a farm two miles long and a half inch wide.
ROGER: What would you grow on a farm that size?
REGGIE: Spaghetti.

JED: Why did the pioneers go West in covered wagons?
NED: I suppose they didn't want to wait forty years for a train.

10

Crazier & Crazier

Two men sat next to each other in the doctor's waiting room.

"I'm aching from arthritis," said one.

"I'm Bent from Birmingham," said the other. "Glad to know you."

JACK: My uncle swallowed a frog.
JILL: Goodness, did it make him sick?
JACK: Sick! He's liable to croak any
minute!

BRIGGS: My uncle disappeared
when he was on safari.
BRAGG: What happened to him?
BRIGGS: My dad says something
he disagreed with ate him.

DORIS: Why do they put telephone
wires so high?
MORRIS: To keep up the conversation.

BUCK: I saw you pushing your
bike to work this morning.
BEN: Yes, I was so late I
didn't have time to get on it.

JESSICA: Is it correct to say that you
water your horse?
MOTHER: Yes, dear.
JESSICA: Then I'm going to milk my
cat.

TILLY: Why did the germ cross
the microscope?
BILLY: To get to the other
slide.

MOTHER: I've told you a million times
not to exaggerate.

FATHER: Where did your mother go?
SON: She's round at the front.
FATHER: I know what she looks like, I want to know where she is.

DAN: My kid brother thought a football coach had four wheels.
STAN: How many does it have?

CALLER (*at door*): Do you believe in the hereafter, madam?
WOMAN: Yes.
CALLER: Well, I'm the landlord, and I'm here after the rent.

BERYL: What happened to the human cannonball at the circus?
CHERYL: He got fired.

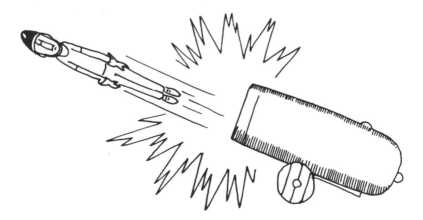

EVE: How old is your brother?

STEVE: He's a year old.

EVE: Well, I've got a dog who's a year old, and he can walk twice as far as your brother.

STEVE: He's got twice as many legs.

CUSTOMER: Waiter, I don't like all the flies in here.

WAITER: Well, just point out the ones you don't like and I'll have them put out.

FATHER: Who gave you that black eye?

JACK: Nobody—I had to fight for it.

LEE: What can run across the floor, but has no legs?

DEE: Water.

AUNTIE: Come on, Billy, dear, eat your cabbage, it's good for growing children.

BILLY: I don't want to grow any children.

DOCTOR: You need glasses.

PATIENT: How can you tell?

DOCTOR: I knew as soon as you came in the window.

MILLY: What are you writing?

MOLLY: I'm writing a letter to myself.

MILLY: What does it say?

MOLLY: How do I know—I won't get it till tomorrow.

MOTHER: Tommy, did you fall down with your good pants on?

TOMMY: Yes, Mom, I didn't have time to take them off.

107

NOAH (*to his son Ham who is fishing*): Go easy on the bait; remember I've only got two worms.

ANGIE: Why do storks lift only one leg?
GEORGIE: If they lifted the other leg they'd fall over.

WYNN: Whenever I'm down in the dumps, I buy new clothes.
LEN: So that's where you get them!

POLICEMAN: I'm afraid I'm going to lock you up for the night.
HOOLIGAN: Why—what's the charge?
POLICEMAN: Oh, there's no charge— it's all part of the service.

DINER: Waiter, this meat isn't fit for a pig.

WAITER: I'll take it back, sir, and bring you some that is.

FANNY (*shaking her husband*): Manny, I heard a mouse squeak.

MANNY: What do you want me to do—oil it?

HOTEL MANAGER: Well, sir, did you enjoy your stay with us?

GUEST: Yes, but it seems hard leaving the place so soon after buying it.

MRS. GRAY: My husband beats me up every morning.

MRS. DAY: How terrible!

MRS. GRAY: Yes, he gets up at seven and I get up at eight.

PAT: How did you manage to crash your car?

MATT: You see that ditch over there?

PAT: Yes.

MATT: Well, I didn't.

Learn from the mistakes of others—you can't live long enough to make them all by yourself.

TRAMP: I haven't had more than one meal this week, lady.

FAT LADY: How I wish I had your willpower!

TED: Did you say your dog's bark was worse than his bite?

NED: Yes.

TED: Then, for heaven's sake, don't let him bark—he just bit me!

CHARLIE: Why does it rain, Dad?

DAD: To make the grass and the flowers grow.

CHARLIE: Well, why does it rain on the pavement?

MOLLY: Have you heard the latest? It's all over the building!

MILLY: What's all over the building?

MOLLY: The roof.

DORIS: Now that we're engaged, I hope you'll give me a ring.
HORACE: Of course, what's your number?

POLICEMAN: Here—why are you trying to cross the road in this dangerous place? There's a zebra crossing just a few yards up the road.
PEDESTRIAN: Well, I hope he's having better luck than I am.

MAVIS: Does your cat have fleas?
TOOTS: Don't be silly, cats don't have fleas; they have kittens.

KEITH: Don't you think I sing with feeling?
MAISIE: No—if you had any feeling, you wouldn't sing.

VISITOR TO FARM: Do you know how long cows should be milked?
FARMER: The same as short ones.

The bus was crowded, and as one more man tried to get on, the passengers wouldn't let him board.

"It's too crowded," they shouted. "Who do you think you are?"

"I'm the driver," he said.

FRAN: My sister is black and blue, because she puts on cold cream, face cream, wrinkle cream, vanishing cream, hair cream and skin cream every night.
RHODA: But why does that make her black and blue?
FRAN: She keeps slipping out of bed.

PATIENT: You were right when you said you'd have me on my feet and walking in no time.

DOCTOR: That's good; when did you start walking?

PATIENT: When I got your bill— I had to sell my car to pay it.

ALBERT: Darling, when we are married, do you think you'll be able to live on my income?

ALVA: I think so, darling, but what will you live on?

GRACIE: The trouble with you is you're always wishing for something you don't have.

TRACY: What else is there to wish for?

SIDNEY: Show me a tough guy and I'll
   show you a coward.
SAM: Well, I'm a tough guy.
SIDNEY: I'm a coward.

   NEIGHBOR: Your daughter is only
      four and can spell her name
      backwards? What's her name?
   PROUD MOTHER: Ada.

   "Mommy—it's getting very hot in
here—can I come out?"
   "Certainly not! Do you want the
fire to spread to the rest of the
house?"

11

Look Out!

In the snake house at the zoo, one snake said to another: "Are we supposed to be poisonous?"
"Why?"
"Well, I just bit my lip."

ROGER: Oh, he's a friendly dog!
He'll eat off your hand.
LODGER: That's what I'm afraid of.

AUNTIE: Well, Gordon, suppose there were only two pieces of cake left—a large piece and a small one. Which piece would you give to your brother?

GORDON: Do you mean my big brother or my little one?

EFFIE: I've just swallowed a bone.

MOTHER: Are you choking?

EFFIE: No, I'm serious.

Goofy Gus had a rope hanging from a tree outside his window.

"What's that for?" asked his brother.

"It's my weather forecaster," said Gus. "When it moves, it's windy, and when it's wet, it's raining."

SHOP OWNER: Yes, madam, these are the same pork pies we've had for years.

CUSTOMER: Could you show me some you've had more recently, please?

JACKSON: There's one word that describes my wife—temperamental.

JONES: In what way?

JACKSON: She's fifty percent temper and fifty percent mental!

116

The trumpet player had been blasting away all day, when there was a knock on his door.

"I live next door to you," he explained. "Do you know I work nights?"

"No," said the trumpet player, "but if you hum a few bars, I'll get the melody."

JOHN: Why is Sunday the strongest day?

JOAN: Because all the others are *week*days.

STAN: What are you taking for your cold?

SID: What will you give me?

Visiting the modern art museum, a lady turned to an attendant standing nearby.

"This," she said, "I suppose, is one of those hideous representations you call modern art?"

"No, madam," replied the attendant. "That one's called a mirror."

Think of a number between one and twenty. Double it, subtract eighteen, add one, subtract the number you started with, close your eyes. . . . Dark, isn't it!

TEACHER: Yes, Theodore, what is it?
THEODORE: I don't want to alarm you, Miss Bates, but my dad said if I didn't get better marks, someone was going to get a licking.

HUSBAND: You didn't have a rag on your back when I married you.
WIFE: Well, I've certainly got plenty now.

TEACHER: David, this is the fifth day this week you've had to stay in after school. What have you to say for yourself?
DAVID: I'm certainly glad it's Friday.

AL: Why can't two elephants go into a swimming pool at the same time?
SAL: Because they have only one pair of trunks.

Dustin's mother was worried about the health of her neighbor.

"Dustin," she said, "run and ask how old Mrs. Jones is."

Soon Dustin was back. "Mrs. Jones was very annoyed," he said. "She said it was none of your business how old she is."

Hickory dickory dock—
Three mice ran up the clock—
The clock struck one—
But the other two managed to get
    away!

MOTHER: How did you get Wayne to take his medicine without protest?
FATHER: I shot it into him with a water pistol.

Two Indians were watching distant smoke signals. When they were finished, one Indian turned to the other and said, "We have to do something about Little Big Horse. His spelling is something awful."

Do you know how to make a slow horse fast?
No—do you?
Yes—don't give him anything to eat.

> MRS. HIGGINS: I'm sorry to bring you out on such a terrible night, Doctor.
> DOCTOR: That's all right. I had to call at a house down the road, so I thought I'd kill two birds with one stone.

"Waiter, there's a twig in my soup."

"Just a moment, sir, I'll call the branch manager."

FRANK: What would I have to give you to get a little kiss?
ZAZA: Chloroform.

DOCTOR: I'm sorry to have to tell you that you may have rabies, and it could prove fatal.
PATIENT: Well, Doctor, please give me pencil and paper.
DOCTOR: To make your will?
PATIENT: No—to make a list of people I want to bite.

Have you heard the one about quicksand? It takes a long time to sink in.

FRANK: Am I the first man
  you've ever kissed?
SUE: You might be—your face
  looks familiar.

  "What are you eating,
Sonny?"
  "An apple."
  "Better look out for worms."
  "Let the worms look out for
themselves."

What did the traffic lights say to
the sports car?
"Don't look now, I'm changing."

EFFIE: My aunt was very embarrassed
  when she was asked to take off her
  mask at the party.
TESSIE: Why was that?
EFFIE: She wasn't wearing one.

"How dare you spit in front of my wife?"

"Why, was it her turn?"

ANGRY MAN: I'll teach you to throw stones at my greenhouse.

LITTLE HORROR: I wish you would—I keep missing it.

"I've got a nasty pain in my right foot, Doctor."

"I shouldn't worry—it's just old age."

"Well, why doesn't the other one hurt—I've had that just as long."

MONTY: Is it really bad luck to have a black cat follow you?

MIKE: Well, it depends on whether you're a man or a mouse.

LECTURER (*to Chairman*): May I sit on your right hand?

CHAIRMAN: You may—but I'll need it later to ring the bell with.

Index

Aaron, 70
Absence (from school), 68
Absent-minded professor, 64
Accident, 26
Ada, 114
Adam, 101; and Eve, 68
Adoption, 67
Ads, 15
Age, 77, 120, 124
Alarm clock, 25
Ancestors, 30
Angina, acute, 18
Anglers, 94
Annoyances, 90
Appearance, 85
Apple, 123
Arab, 21
Arithmetic, 97, 118; class, 87
Army, 22
Arrows, 45
Art, 71; modern, 118
Arthritis, 103
Artist, 65
Attendance, 90
Author, 83

Baby, 74
Backseat drivers, 26
Bait, 108
Baldness, 77
Ball, 12
Ballet, 64
Band, 18; town, 95
Bank, 53; manager, 33
Barbed wire fence, 33
Barber, 17, 86
Bark, 110
Bath, 75; room, 8
Bed, 57, 86, 112
Beer, 81
Bells, 42
Bible, 36, 101
Bicycle, 104; pump, 35
Bill, 34
Bird seed, 73
Birth, 83
Birthday presents, 44, 46
Bites, 85, 90, 110
Black-and-blue, 112
Black: cat, 124; eye, 101, 106

Blinds, 25
Boarding school, 99
Boasting, 30
Boats, 41
Books, 83
Bores, 43
Boss, 10, 14, 18, 59, 84
Boys and girls, 90, 111, 122, 123
Breakfast, 38
Bride, 63; groom, 63
Brothers, 50, 106, 116
Building, 110
Bull, 59
Buns, currant, 51
Burglar, 42
Bus, 11, 112
Butcher, 19, 22, 32, 51
Button, 58

Cabbage, 84, 107
Caesar, Julius, 76
Cake, 50, 116
Calculator, 19
Camel, 21
Camera, 86
Camp, nudist, 96
Canaries, 64
Cannibal, 38, 79
Cannonball, human, 105
Captain, 101
Car, 7, 17, 22, 26, 27, 28, 30, 45, 48, 63, 109
Cards, pack of, 59
Carpentry, 27
Cat, 37, 52, 80, 91, 104, 111; black, 124; family, 15
Cemetery, 14, 93
Census, 77
Centipede, 57
Cereal, 13
Chairman, 124
Charge, 108
Cheating, 80
Cheeks, 84
Chess, 18
Chickens, 12, 52, 55, 56, 92; soup, 81
Child, unwanted, 41
Children, growing, 107

Chloroform, 122
Choking, 116
Chop, karate, 36
Christianity, 79
Christmas presents, 77
Church collection, 45
Circus, 105
Class, bottom of, 82
Cloakroom, 55
Clock, 120; alarm, 25; grandfather, 58
Clothes, 108, 119
Coach, 105
Coat, 74
Coffee, 35, 88
Cold, 117
Comb, 77
Comedian, 50
Concorde, 56
Conversation, 104
Cooking, 52, 65
Corn: ear of, 82; flakes, 13
Coughing, 14
Covered wagons, 102
Coward, 114
Cows, 42, 112
Crab, 9
Crutches, 86
Curtains, 51

Dance, 67
Dating, 32, 34, 64
Days, 38; strongest, 117
Death, 82
Decorator, 57
Dentist, 15, 28
Diet, reducing, 48, 60, 102
Dinner, 52
Ditch, 109
Doctor, 9, 10, 18, 33, 35, 37, 51, 59, 75, 83, 86, 93, 98, 101, 107, 113, 121, 122, 124; waiting room of, 103
Dodge City, 42
Dog, 10, 14, 16, 30, 31, 59, 62, 63, 66, 73, 106, 110, 115; license, 16, 54; meat, 92
Doll, 44
Dolphins, 45

Dracula, 31
Dress, 17, 23, 42; shop, 36
Driver, bus, 112
Driving, 50; *also see Car*
Duck, 34
Dumps, down in the, 108
Dust, 36

Ears, 14, 42
Earth, 11
Eclipse, solar, 98
Editor, news, 94
Eggs, 33, 52
Electric blanket, 72
Elephants, 67, 119
Encyclopedia, 8, 29
Escape, 54
Eve, Adam and, 68
Excuse, 68
Eye, black, 101, 106

Face, 73
Fame, 62
Family, 30; album, 74
Farm, 59, 102
Farmer, 37, 92
Fashion, 93
Fasting, 121
Fat, 36, 49, 55, 69, 110
Father's footsteps, 42
Feeling, 111
Feet, 124; flat, 35
Fence, 44
Fiddle, 40
Fight, 26
Film, 86; star, 87
Fingers, 45
Fire, 114; man, 80
Fish, 94
Fisherman, 70
Fishing, 94, 108; permit, 47
Flat: feet, 35; tire, 88
Fleas, 14, 111
Flies, 106
Fly, 51; in soup, 13
Foolproof, 25
Fools, 16
Football, 94; coach, 105
Footsteps, 42
Foreigners, 19
Fraud, 63
French lessons, 67
Friday, 119
Frog, 104
Furniture, 47

Gadget, 25
Gangster, 66
Garage door, 17
Garbage, 20
Garden, 83
Gentleman, 49
Germs, 14, 104
Giraffe, 26
Girls, boys and, 90, 111, 122, 123
Glasses, 85, 107
Goat, 9
Goldfish, 12
Goofy Gus, 43, 48, 116
Grades, 118
Grandfather clock, 58
Grandma, 85, 100
Gravity, 62
Greenhouse, 124
Guarantee, 17
Guards, 25
Guilt complex, 89

Ham, 108
Hand, 124
Hankies, 77
Hardware store, 26
Hat, 55, 84
Hay, making, 37
Head, standing on, 95
Health, 14, 120
Hearse, 26
Heart operation, 83
Hereafter, 105
Hickory dickory dock, 120
Hi-jacking, 56
Hold-up, 71, 72
Holes, knot, 98
Homework, 15
Honesty, 85
Horns, 42
Horse, 44, 76, 104, 121
Hospital, 93
Hotdog, 59
Hotel manager, 109
Hot water, 18
Hours, shorter, 63
House calls, 121
Husband, 24; *also see Marriage, Wife*
Hygiene, 35

I, letter, 90
Identity, mistaken, 89

Illness, 51, 59
Imagination, 91
Indians, 121
Indigestion, 30; acid, 16
Indonesia, 70
Ink, 81
Insomnia, 13
Interior decorator, 57
Invitations, 90

Jail, 108
Jakarta, 70
Jam, jar of, 55
Jobs, 20, 41, 59, 84
Judge, 7, 23, 28, 58, 63
Jumping, horse, 44

Kangaroo, 20, 75
Karate chop, 36
Kettle, 93
Kiss, 29, 33, 122, 123
Kittens, 111
Kleptomaniac, 99
Knights, 11
Knotholes, 98

Ladder, 41
Lamb, 22
Landlord, 105
Lassie, 87
Last person on earth, 68
Lateness, 104
Leaves, 47
Lecturer, 124
Lemonade, 61
Lemons, 97
Lent, 38
Leopard, 35
Letter, 81, 107
Liar, 67
Library, 29
License, dog, 54, 96
Life, long, 39
Light, 16
Limp, 53
Lion, 19
London, 25, 56
Long distance telephone, 66
Luck, bad, 124
Lying low, 60

Magicians, 83
Manager: branch, 122; office, 85, 99
Manners, 32, 41, 49, 60

Marks, 118
Marriage, 53, 68, 74, 92, 113, 119
Mask, 123
Match, 81
Math, 13, 45, 118
Measles, 33, 46, 88, 98
Meatballs, 89
Medicine, 25, 120
Memory, 22
Menu, 59, 69
Mice, 91, 120; *also see Mouse*
Microscope, 104
Middle Ages, 11
Milk, 70
Mind, 95
Mint, 82
Mirror, 118; shaving, 22
Miser, 72
Missionary, 38, 79
Mistakes, 109
Mittens, 80
Modern art, 118
Money, 67, 71, 72, 82
Months, 12
Moon, 24, 55
Moses, 70
Mother, 94, 98, 100, 102, 105; in-law, 65, 84; Nature, 96
Motorist, 26, 27, 38; *also see Car*
Mouse, 109, 124; trap, 26; *also see Mice*
Movies, 13, 23
Mower, 25
Mud, 9
Muffler, 57
Muscle, 101
Musician, 117

Nail-biting, 47
Nativity, 44
Nature, Mother, 96
Neighbor, 52, 53, 120
Nets, 70
Newlyweds, 48, 63
Newspaper, 94
Newton, Isaac, 62
Niagara Falls, 27
Noah, 108
Nose, 77
Nudist camp, 96
Nurse, 14, 19

Oatmeal, 86
Office, 10; boy, 18; manager, 85, 99
Oil, 63; check, 86; tank, 20
Ointment, 97
One-eyed man, 54
One-way street, 27, 45
Overcoat, 57
Oversleeping, 18

Pain, 30
Painting, 65, 71
Parakeets, 64
Parcel, 43
Parrot, 57
Party, 90, 123
Patient, 33, 35, 51, 61, 89, 93, 97, 113, 122
Pedestrian, 45, 111
Pen, 29
Pencil, 29
Penny, 67
Pet shop, 35
Photograph, 34
Photosynthesis, 47
Piano, 40; lessons, 45; tuner, 53
Pie, 42, 43, 116
Pig, 19, 48, 92, 109
Pigeons, 74
Pillowcase, 52
Pills, 59; sleeping, 37
Pilot, 56
Pine, knotty, 98
Pioneers, 102
Pistol, water, 120
Plant, 87
Plumbers, 27
Poet, 43
Police, 88; man, 26, 27, 42, 45, 46, 47, 108, 111; station, 48
Pool, swimming, 119
Postman, 43, 62
Post office, 77
Prince, 29
Principal, 90
Prisoner, 7, 23, 54, 58, 63, 98
Procrastination, 89
Professor, 66; absent-minded, 67
Proverb, 68
Psychiatrist, 51, 89; *also see Doctor*

Pulse, 19
Puppies, 41
Pyramids, 23

Quicksand, 122

Rabies, 122
Races: boat, 41; horse, 54
Rags, 119
Rain, 74, 110
Receptionist, 93
Refinery, 41
Religion, 38
Rent, 105
Reporter, 94
Rheumatism, 75
Rhinoceros, 68
Rice Krispies, 13
Riding backwards, 64
Ring, 111
River, 86
Road, mountain, 50
Robbery, 9, 23, 60, 85
Roof, 41, 110
Roots, square, 87
Rope, 97, 116
Rover, 46
Rust, 22

Saddle, 76
Safari, 35, 104
Safecracker, 9
Sailors, 66
Saint Bernard, 73
Salad, 58
Salesman, 28
Sausages, 51
Scaffolding, 78
Scale, 69
Scarf, 17
School, 16, 69, 82, 96, 119
Scruples, 33
Seasonings, 22
Secretary, 87, 99
Serial, 13
Sheriff, 42
Ships, 101
Shirt, 100
Shoes, 24
Shot, 81
Shower, 34
Signs, 27, 28, 35, 46, 48
Simple Simon, 52
Singing, 111
Skeleton, 79

Sleep, 13, 18, 32, 89
Sleeping pills, 37
Smiling, 76
Smoke signals, 121
Smoking in bed, 75
Snake, 11, 115
Soap: flakes, 38; oatmeal, 86
Soccer, 12
Solar eclipse, 98
Soup, 40, 81, 122
Spaghetti, 102
Spelling, 121
Spit, 124
Spoon, 24
Stamp, 77
Stealing, 85
Steam roller, 72
Steel wool, 33
Store, hardware, 26
Stork, 82, 108
Strangers, 32, 66
Strike, 28, 63, 82
String, balls of, 55
Students, 67
Studying, 36
Success, 68
Suit, 87, 93
Suitor, 53
Sunday, 38, 117; school, 36
Sunglasses, 22
Superstition, 88
Surprise, 44, 73
Sweater, 73
Swimming, 40; pool, 119

Table: manners, 32, 60;
    tennis, 86
Tail, 63
Tailor, 87
Tarzan, 39
Taxes, 83, 96

Tea, 14, 24; iced, 81
Teachers, 16, 23, 24, 60, 80,
    90, 118; *also see School*
Teeth, 80
Telegram, 99
Telephone, 66, 89, 100;
    wires, 104
Temper, 116
Tennis racket, 25
Texas, 27
Theatre, 13
Thief, 60
Thunderstorm, 51
Tickets, 78; movie, 23;
    zoo, 24
Time, 25, 79
Tire, flat, 88
Toad, 29
Toaster, 72
Toboggan, 43
Tongue, 60
Tonsillitis, 61
Tooth, 28
Tough guy, 114
Tourist, 76
Train, 21, 26, 64, 102
Tramp, 31, 85, 110
Tricks, 83
Trousers, 65
Trumpet player, 117
Trunks, 119
TV, 44, 85
21-gun salute, 83
Typing, 99

Ugliness, 63
Umbrella, 74
Undertaker, 51

Violin, 93; case, 66
Volkswagen, 27

Waiter, 10, 13, 16, 20, 30,
    35, 36, 58, 59, 69, 72, 88,
    92, 106, 109, 122
Waking up, 101, 109
Walking, 113
Washing machine, 85
Watch, 34; wrist, 15, 58, 83
Water, 102, 106; pistol, 120;
    skiing, 40
Wealth, 31, 75
Weather, 28, 34, 56;
    forecasting, 116
Wedding, 84
Weekdays, 117
Weightlifting, 95
West, 102
Whales, 84
Whiskers, 40
Wholesome, 70
Wife, 116, 124; *also see
    Husband, Marriage*
Wig, 70
Willpower, 110
Window, 88
Wishing, 113
Wool: ball of, 80; steel, 33
Work, 10, 38, 59, 99
Workers, 82
World, 87
Worms, 42, 47, 108, 123
Wrestling match, 85
Wristwatch, 15, 58, 83
Writer, 25, 62

X-ray, 53

Year, 38
Yokel, 20

Zebra crossing, 111
Zoo, 24, 54, 115